THE SCIENCE OF

MOTORCYCLE

RACING

BY MARCIA AMIDON LUSTED

CONSULTANT:
PAUL OHMANN, PH.D.
ASSOCIATE PROFESSOR AND CHAIR OF PHYSICS
UNIVERSITY OF ST. THOMAS, MINNESOTA

CAPSTONE PRESS
a capstone imprint

Velocity Books are published by Capstone Press,
1710 Roe Crest Drive, North Mankato, Minnesota 56003
www.capstonepub.com

Library of Congress Cataloging-in-Publication Data
Lusted, Marcia Amidon, author.
The science of motorcycle racing / by Marcia Amidon Lusted.
    pages cm.—(Velocity—the science of speed)
  Summary: "Describes the science concepts involved in several types of motorcycle racing"— Provided by publisher.
  Audience: 10–14.
  Audience: Grades 4 to 6.
  Includes bibliographical references and index.
  ISBN 978-1-4765-3912-6 (library binding)
  ISBN 978-1-4765-5195-1 (pbk.)
  ISBN 978-1-4765-6060-1 (ebook PDF)
  1. Motorcycle racing—Juvenile literature. 2. Motorcycles—Juvenile literature. I. Title. II. Series: Velocity (Capstone Press)
  GV1060.L87 2014
  796.7'5—dc23   2013026807

Editorial Credits
Adrian Vigliano, editor; Kyle Grenz, designer; Laura Manthe, production specialist

Photo Credits
Alamy: Andrew Orchard, 13 (top), The Photolibrary Wales/Andrew Orchard, 36; Courtesy of American Honda Motor Co., Inc., 12 (top), 14, 18, 19, 24; Newscom: Actionplus/Tim Williams, 39 (top), Cal Sport Media/Mat Gdowski, 41, EPA/Maxim Shipenkov, 37 (bottom), Icon SMI/Brian Ekart, 42-43 (top), imago sportfotodienst, 20-21 (bottom), ZUMA Press/Mat Gdowski, 39 (bottom); Shutterstock: Ahmad Faizal Yahya, 35, Artit Thongchuea, 38, B.Stefanov, 4-5, CHEN WS, 7, Chris Roselli, 32 (bottom), David Acosta Allely, cover, Diego Barbieri, 21 (top), F.C.G., 11, fotographic1980, (background, throughout), Gustavo Miguel Fernandes, 28 (top), haak78, 12-13 (bottom), Ilya Andriyanov, 15 (bottom), Jemny, 8, Marcel Jancovic, 23 (top), 25, Natursports, 16-17, nexus 7, 32 (top), PhotoStock10, 27, Racefotos2008, 5 (top), 30-31, Steve Mann, 42-43 (bottom), TachePhoto, 15 (top), taelove7, 37 (top), Ventura, 34, VVKSAM, 22, 23 (bottom), Yuri2010, 44-45, zhangyouyang, 28-29 (bottom); Wikimedia: AndroidCat, 33

Printed in the United States of America in Stevens Point, Wisconsin.
092013   007767WZS14

TABLE OF CONTENT

Feel the Power

Engines roar. Tires spin up dirt clouds. Motorcycle riders in their bright helmets and gear dart and weave around the track. They climb hills and plunge down again. All around the track, fans cheer and shout. The smell of exhaust drifts through the air. These motorcycles are not made to be driven on the street. They are fine-tuned machines for racing.

Motorcycle racing is more than excitement and thrills. It's also science in action. Science affects everything from tires grabbing the track surface to how fast a motorcycle travels.

FACT
The first gas-powered motorcycle was invented in 1885. Gottlieb Daimler created it by attaching an engine to a wooden bicycle frame.

Chapter 1:

Designed for Speed

AMAZING MACHINES

A motorcycle is a lot like a bicycle. But in a motorcycle the engine provides power instead of human legs. The power goes to the back wheel. It is often transferred by a chain drive. The handlebars connect to the front fork of the motorcycle frame. They steer the bike and may also have some of the controls for the rider. Other controls are found near the foot pedals. **Suspension** cushions the rider from bumps. The tires create **friction** with the road, helping the bike move and stick to the track.

① ② ③ ④

A racing motorcycle has the same basic parts as a motorcycle driven on the street.

A simple machine does work with only one movement. There are six kinds of simple machines: lever, pulley, inclined plane, wheel and **axle**, wedge, and screw. A motorcycle uses three of these, so it is actually a complex machine.

suspension—the system of springs and shock absorbers that absorbs a motorcycle's up-and-down movements
friction—one surface rubbing against another
axle—a bar in the center of a wheel around which a wheel turns

A motorcycle has two wheels and axles. When the axle is turned by the engine's power, the wheel also turns.

Handlebars are levers. A lever is an arm that pivots against a point called a fulcrum. The two motorcycle handlebars are levers that make it easier to turn the fork, which holds the front wheel.

① seat
② rear wheel
③ muffler
④ rear brakes
⑤ handlebars with controls
⑥ gas tank
⑦ front fairing
⑧ front suspension
⑨ front fork
⑩ front brakes
⑪ front wheel
⑫ fairing (frame is underneath)
⑬ engine
⑭ foot rest

The chain drive is a pulley. The chain drive connects the engine with the rear drive wheel. As the engine turns a gear at one end of a chain loop, that chain also turns another gear on the back motorcycle wheel.

A motorcycle needs friction to move. Friction that happens when motorcycle tires stick to the track surface is called traction. Tire grooves, or tread, can be bumpy, which help create traction on rough surfaces like dirt or rocks. Tires can also be smoother, which helps increase traction on smooth, dry surfaces. Racers use different treads depending on what kind of track they will ride on.

MOMENTUM = MASS X VELOCITY

Once an object begins moving, it wants to keep moving in a straight line because of **momentum**. In fact, the faster a motorcycle goes, the less it wants to turn. This is also because the motorcycle has momentum. Momentum equals mass times velocity. Mass is the amount of matter that makes up a motorcycle and its rider. Velocity is how fast the motorcycle is moving in a certain direction.

AIR MOVEMENT

Motorcycles are also built to be **aerodynamic** for less **air resistance**. If the shape of a motorcycle is sleek, the air slips around it and the motorcycle can go fast. If the shape is not aerodynamic, air doesn't flow smoothly, which slows down the motorcycle.

momentum—the property of a moving object equal to its mass times its velocity
aerodynamic—built to move easily through the air
air resistance—the force the air exerts on an object moving through it

BIG POWER

A racing motorcycle relies on its engine to supply explosive power. A motorcycle engine is a combustion engine.

A 4-stroke combustion engine works like this:

fuel-air mixture

valve

First stroke
Intake: The intake valve opens and fuel and air are released into the combustion chamber.

piston

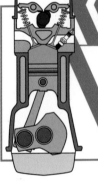

Second stroke
Compression: The intake valve closes. The piston moves up to compress the fuel and air.

spark plug

Third stroke
Power: A spark plug creates a spark and ignites the mixture. Energy is released from the fuel and air. The energy forces the piston down, moving other parts in the engine.

Fourth stroke
Exhaust: The piston moves up again and the exhaust valve opens. Gases are pushed out of the combustion chamber.

1 Gasoline and air ignite, or combust, using a spark from a spark plug.

2 The combustion makes pistons move up and down.

3 The pistons turn a crankshaft.

4 The spinning crankshaft moves the chain through the motorcycle's transmission. **Torque** makes the chain move and the back wheel turn, so the motorcycle moves. The amount of torque determines how fast the motorcycle's back wheel turns and how fast it goes.

FACT

Too much torque makes it hard for a motorcycle to go around corners. If the rear wheel is turning too fast, the tire doesn't have enough contact with the road surface to hold on through a corner.

torque—a turning force used to rotate or spin an object

TURNING CORNERS

In order to turn a motorcycle's front wheel and move around a corner, riders use forces such as **gravity** and friction.

When the rider turns the handlebars, momentum tends to make the motorcycle stay straight. The rider must lean on the motorcycle toward the inside of the curve.

gravity—a force that pulls objects toward the center of Earth

No Brakes

In speedway and grasstrack racing, the motorcycles don't have brakes. Racers create friction by sliding their motorcycles sideways on corners. Sliding slows down the bikes. But riders can't slow down too much. They must learn to keep enough speed to make it out of the corner and back onto a fast straightaway.

Speedway racing

The rider then uses gravity, friction, and a force called the **normal force** to make the motorcycle turn. The normal force pushes up from the track, perpendicular to the surface. The rider must be aware of these forces to make the motorcycle go where he or she wants it to.

normal force—the force that pushes up on objects that are in contact with the ground

Chapter 2:
At the Track

TO THE LIMIT

Motorcycle racing takes place on all sorts of tracks and surfaces. Road racing takes place on asphalt tracks. Motocross racing takes place on off-road surfaces such as dirt, mud, grass, and sand. Each track's surface makes a different kind of traction.

Motocross tracks are meant to be challenging. They have many changes in elevation, from low points to steep hills. These changes require a motorcycle to deal with **adhesion limit**.

Imagine a racer trying to climb a steep hill. Halfway up, the bike's back wheel begins to spin uselessly. There isn't enough friction between the back wheel and the track surface. The motorcycle has reached its adhesion limit and can't stick to the surface. No matter how much power the back wheel gets, it can't climb that steep hill. In this situation the motorcycle can't transmit enough weight to the ground to use its power.

adhesion limit—the limit of a motorcycle's ability to stick to the ground

People love the many different kinds of motorcycle racing. Some races are especially difficult because of the low levels of traction found on certain track surfaces. Which type of race do you think would be trickiest for racers?

Hill climb:
Races take place on a steep hill or a mountain.

Cross-Country Rally:
Includes hundreds of miles on off-road, open terrain such as deserts.

Hare scramble:
Tracks go through different types of rugged natural terrain such as woods, hills, and deserts.

Supermoto:
Combines road racing and motocross. The surface includes both asphalt and dirt sections.

HITTING THE BRAKES

In motorcycle racing, braking is just as important as speed. Braking the wrong way, especially on corners or hills, can force the motorcycle into unexpected positions.

When a motorcycle rider brakes, the bike slows down. Weight is transferred to the front wheel from the back wheel, even though there are brakes on both wheels. The **center of gravity** (cg) moves toward the front. The movement of the center of gravity can make the motorcycle tip forward. If the bike tips too far on its front wheel, the rider may flip over the handlebars.

Wheelbase Makes a Difference

The distance between the two axles on a motorcycle is called the wheelbase. Motorcycles with a shorter wheelbase and a high center of gravity are easier to handle when cornering and braking. Motorcycles with a long wheelbase and a low center of gravity can speed up and slow down with less danger of toppling. But bikes with a long wheelbase are harder to handle when cornering and braking.

FACT

Motorcycles are designed to help riders stay balanced. Designers keep the heaviest part of a motorcycle—the engine—as low as possible on bike frames.

BALANCING ACT

Braking is even trickier when racing around corners. Riders must understand angles and arcs. Angles help riders know how sharp a corner is. Riders use arcs to understand the distance around a corner.

Riders try to move through each corner in as small of an arc as possible. By tracing a smaller arc through the corner, riders keep their motorcycles as stable as possible and lose less speed. They do this by braking before the corner and cutting close to the inside point, or the apex. Then they speed up again while exiting the corner.

The rider is also trying to overcome **inertia**, because objects try to resist a change in motion. Gravity and the normal force are trying to make the rider's motorcycle fall over inside the curve.

Banked Turns

Many corners on racetracks, especially oval tracks, are banked. Banked turns are built to slope from a high point on the outside edge down toward the track. A banked curve allows the motorcycle to take the turn at a faster speed than a turn on flat ground.

inertia—tendency of an object to remain either at rest or in motion unless affected by an outside force

JUMPS AND STUNTS

Some tracks cause motorcycles to go over jumps and become airborne. Gravity makes an airborne bike follow a **trajectory** though the air. The rider must work to control the bike's position until gravity pulls it back down to the track surface. The faster the motorcycle is going when it hits the jump, the farther it will go.

Some riders can flip their bikes. Increasing speed while jumping can make the motorcycle rotate backward and tip up. Using the brakes lowers the front of the bike. The rider also adjusts his or her center of gravity and uses the handlebars and foot rests to tilt the bike.

trajectory—a curved path of an object as it flies through the air

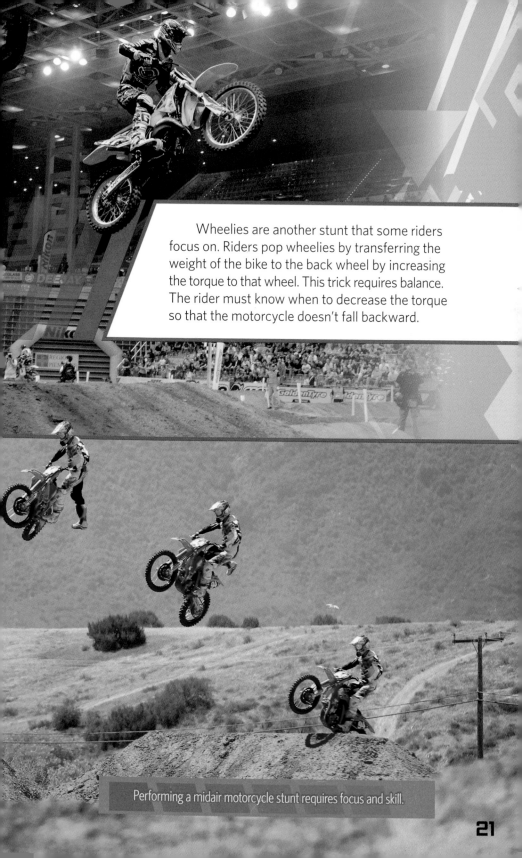

Wheelies are another stunt that some riders focus on. Riders pop wheelies by transferring the weight of the bike to the back wheel by increasing the torque to that wheel. This trick requires balance. The rider must know when to decrease the torque so that the motorcycle doesn't fall backward.

Performing a midair motorcycle stunt requires focus and skill.

BALANCING FORCES

The forces that work to keep a motorcycle moving and cornering quickly can also work against the driver. If a bike's front wheel hits an obstacle such as a rock, the rider's momentum can become dangerous.

Because the rider still has momentum, he or she continues to move while flying over the handlebars. The wrong balance of gravity, friction, and the normal force can also tip the bike over onto the rider during a corner.

There are two common kinds of crashes in motorcycle racing. Low-side crashes happen when bike wheels lose traction, which means the friction force was too small. If too much traction is lost, a fall occurs, causing the bike and rider to slide across the track.

In a high-side crash the back wheel loses traction and then gets it back. Quickly gaining traction again creates a huge momentum boost. Sometimes this unexpected boost causes the rider and the motorcycle to cartwheel through the air. When this happens riders can be hit by a cartwheeling bike.

Chapter 3

In It to Win It

BODY POWER

The race begins and a pack of riders takes off on a **supercross** track. As they race up hills, around corners, and plunge down hills, what is taking place in their bodies?

Riding on a motorcycle during any kind of race takes a lot of physical effort. Riders may not be running, turning pedals, or lifting weights. But racing puts huge stress on a rider's heart, lungs, and reactions. Motorcycle racing demands that riders have a great deal of physical stamina.

Racers tend to have strong **aerobic** power. During a race a rider's heart rate rises. Aerobic power helps a rider's heart and lungs endure during a long race. Riders also have strong legs and plenty of gripping power in their hands.

FACT

There are motocross racers in every age group, from young kids all the way to adults older than 50. However, most professional motocross racers retire by their 40s.

supercross—a type of motorcycle race on a dirt track inside a stadium
aerobic—involving exercise that makes the heart and lungs work harder

THE HUMAN MACHINE

A motorcycle racer needs to use many body parts at once to win. Strength, quick reactions, and coordination are required to come out on top.

ARMS
Need strength for controlling handlebars over bumps and for steering.

SPINE
Compresses to help body absorb shock of a bumpy ride.

HEART AND LUNGS
Aerobic power in the heart and lungs provides high levels of energy and blood flow. Energy and blood flow allow movement and endurance for long races.

JOINTS IN KNEES AND ELBOWS
Need flexibility to absorb the shock of bumps.

LEGS AND FEET
Legs must be strong enough to support a standing position. Legs also have strength to shift the center of gravity to maintain balance and control while cornering.

EYES

Must work quickly to process information on the track. The eyes also help to coordinate balance and movement. They work with the hands to create hand-eye coordination.

HANDS

Strength needed for holding handlebars, controlling the throttle to accelerate, and squeezing brakes to slow down. They work with the eyes to create hand-eye coordination.

INJURIES

Like any sport, motorcycle racing can cause injuries. Even well-trained, careful riders run the risk of physcial injuries. The most common injuries include:

SPINE AND JOINTS:
injuries from crushing, overcompression, or extension

WRISTS:
damage from **impact force** in crashes

impact force—a high force applied over a short time as two bodies or objects collide and change momentum

Laying Down

If used correctly, modern brakes should allow riders to stop quickly in a straight line on any surface. But many old bikes had poor brakes and couldn't always stop well. Motorcycle racers used to practice sliding, or laying down, bikes as a method of emergency stopping. This didn't always work well. Tire rubber has much more traction than materials found on the sides of a bike, such as metal or plastic. Sliding on low-traction materials could mean a more uncontrolled, dangerous situation for the rider. Sliding riders often suffered broken bones and other injuries.

HEAD:
injuries from impact force

SHOULDERS:
injuries from twisting or wrenching while controlling the motorcycle

SKIN:
cuts and injuries resulting from the friction of sliding on the track surface. These sliding injuries are often called road rash

BONES:
fractures from impact force in crashes

Chapter 4:
High-Tech Racing Gear

STAYING SAFE

Motorcycle racing can be really dangerous. But with the best equipment available, riders can reduce their chances of being injured in a race.

A good helmet is one of the most important pieces of equipment in motorcycle racing. Modern technology has helped companies develop many different helmets.

All motorcycle helmets need to have a hard shell. A helmet's outer shell is made of carbon fiber. Carbon fiber is a type of plastic with fibers embedded in it to make it stronger. The inside is a padded shell made of polystyrene. Polystyrene is a type of plastic.

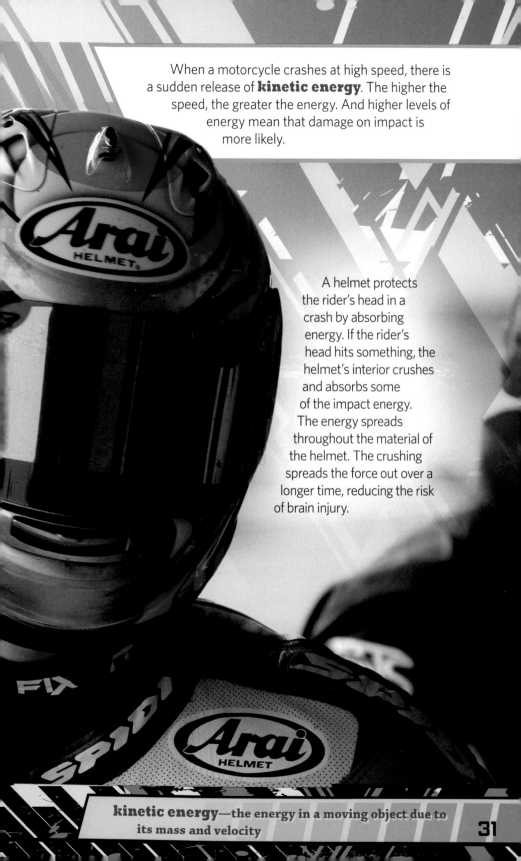

When a motorcycle crashes at high speed, there is a sudden release of **kinetic energy**. The higher the speed, the greater the energy. And higher levels of energy mean that damage on impact is more likely.

A helmet protects the rider's head in a crash by absorbing energy. If the rider's head hits something, the helmet's interior crushes and absorbs some of the impact energy. The energy spreads throughout the material of the helmet. The crushing spreads the force out over a longer time, reducing the risk of brain injury.

kinetic energy—the energy in a moving object due to its mass and velocity

HELMET TYPES

Different types of racing need specialized helmets to keep riders safe. Here are some of the basic categories:

Full Face

A full-face helmet covers the racer's entire head and face, including the base of the skull and the chin. It often has vents for airflow. A flip-up visor protects the eyes.

Motocross

A full-face helmet with longer chin and visor sections. It has a partly open-face section so the rider can wear goggles and also have more airflow during a strenuous race.

Modular or Flip-Up

This helmet is a full-face helmet, but the chin section can be flipped up or removed when the rider doesn't need it. These helmets are designed to be worn for full-face protection during races, and flipped up only when the rider is not racing.

FACT

Motorcycle and car racing helmets are not the same. A car racer's helmet must be fireproof. A motorcycle helmet doesn't need to be fireproof, since the rider won't get trapped inside a burning vehicle.

SUITING UP

How does a motorcycle racer's body stay protected during a race? Protective racing clothing is made out of leather, plastic, fabric, or Kevlar. Racing clothes have padding made from foam, plastic, and carbon fiber. These padded clothes protect the rider from flying debris as well as scrapes and cuts.

Many road racing suits have a speed hump on the back to make them more aerodynamic. The hump also protects the rider's neck during a crash by propping it up.

Kevlar

Kevlar is a man-made fabric. It is five times as strong as the same weight of steel would be. Kevlar is woven in a pattern like tiny interlocking spider webs, which helps make it strong.

Road Racing Suit

shoulder
-has padding and plastic armor

back
-has padding and plastic armor

elbow
-has padding and plastic armor

hip
-has plastic armor

gloves
-made of leather or Kevlar with carbon fiber knuckle protection and pre-curved fingers to make grasping easier

pants
-made of leather or Kevlar

knee
-has armor

boots
-made with plastic caps on toes and ankles

Chapter 5

Track Design

KNOW YOUR SURFACE

Motorcycle racing is very different depending on where it takes place. Outdoor riders must know how factors such as weather can change the track. For example, a damp, cool day will create different levels of friction than a hot, dry day. Here are some common track types along with their features:

Oval track:

- banked corners make it easier to turn at higher speeds
- surface is usually hard-packed dirt

Speedway-racing track

Speedway-racing track:

- oval track made from a loose surface of granite or brick granules
- no asphalt, tar, or hard surfaces allowed
- track is level and often graded between races
- often watered down to prevent dust

Motocross track

Motocross track:

- surface is dirt, mud, sand, and grass, so friction level varies
- natural or artificial hills, jumps, and tight turns

Road racetrack:

- takes place on twisty racetracks with curves in both directions
- some corners are not banked
- surface is asphalt

Road race track

BUILDING A TRACK

Designers have to do a great deal of planning before building a racetrack. They must follow the rules for the specific type of racing the track will be used for. They have to consider safety and speed as they plan the angles for the track's curves. Once all of the plans are in place, it's time to build the track.

The construction of a supercross track in a stadium might look like this:

1 5,000 sheets of plywood or plastic are put down on the stadium's floor to protect it.

2 Five hundred truckloads of dirt weighing about 1.5 million pounds (680, 389 kilograms) are brought into the stadium in dump trucks.

3 Dirt may be watered down if it is too dry. Watering the dirt makes it easier to pack the surface down. If it's too loose, riders won't be able to get enough traction while racing.

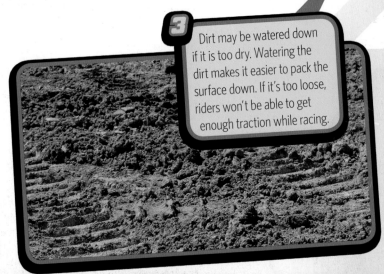

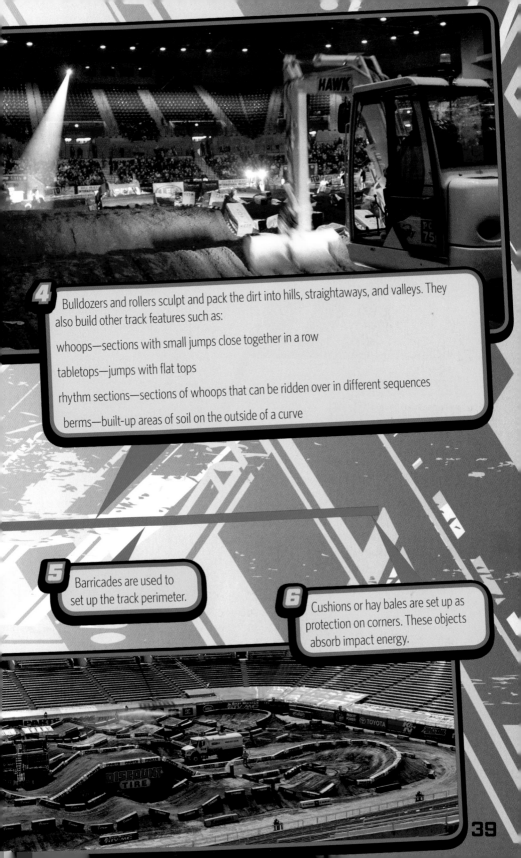

4 Bulldozers and rollers sculpt and pack the dirt into hills, straightaways, and valleys. They also build other track features such as:

whoops—sections with small jumps close together in a row

tabletops—jumps with flat tops

rhythm sections—sections of whoops that can be ridden over in different sequences

berms—built-up areas of soil on the outside of a curve

5 Barricades are used to set up the track perimeter.

6 Cushions or hay bales are set up as protection on corners. These objects absorb impact energy.

BUMPY RIDING

When racing motorcycles on extreme terrain, riders rely on suspensions to help smooth the ride. Suspensions keep tires in contact with the track as much as possible for maximum traction. Suspension also helps to absorb bumps to reduce the impact on the rider.

Front fork suspension

On each side of the front wheel there is a tube that can slide and compress. Some tubes use metal springs to absorb bumps. Others use compressed air instead of springs.

①—┤ triple tree
②—┤ fixed fork
③—┤ hydraulic chamber
④—┤ active fork
⑤—┤ axle

Rear suspension

The swing arm connects the back wheel and the motorcycle frame. The arm pivots on both ends, and one or two shock absorbers are located in the middle of the arm.

The suspensions allow the motorcycle to absorb the bumps and jolts of the track surface. Adjusting the suspensions can help create a smoother ride.

DRAG RACING

Drag motorcycles are designed to accelerate as fast as possible down a short, straight track. Drag motorcycles have a wide back tire to create as much traction as possible.

A drag engine is so powerful that it can push the bike into a wheelie. To keep both wheels on the ground, some drag bikes use a wheelie bar. A wheelie bar is a long frame that extends out behind the rear wheel.

Future of Motorcycle Gear

Motorcycle safety gear keeps advancing along with bike technology. Devices such as airbag suits are becoming more common. Airbag suits detect when a crash occurs and inflate to protect the rider's body. Airbag-suit technology could advance further to keep riders even safer. Some designers have imagined an airbag suit that inflates a safety ball around the rider in less than one second!

adhesion limit (ad-HEE-shuhn LIM-it)—the limit of a motorcycle's ability to stick to the ground

aerobic (ayr-OH-bik)—involving exercise that makes the heart and lungs work harder

aerodynamic (ayr-oh-dy-NA-mik)—built to move easily through the air

air resistance (AIR ri-ZISS-tuhnss)—the force the air exerts on an object moving through it

axle (AK-suhl)—a bar in the center of a wheel around which a wheel turns

center of gravity (SEN-tur UHV GRAV-uh-tee)—the point at which an object can balance

friction (FRIK-shuhn)—one surface rubbing against another

gravity (GRAV-uh-tee)—a force that pulls objects toward the center of Earth

impact force (IM-pakt FORSS)—a high force applied over a short time as two bodies or objects collide and change momentum

inertia (in-UR-shuh)—tendency of an object to remain either at rest or in motion unless affected by an outside force

kinetic energy (ki-NET-ik EN-ur-jee)—the energy in a moving object due to its mass and velocity

momentum (moh-MEN-tuhm)—the property of a moving object equal to its mass times its velocity

normal force (NOHR-muhl FORSS)—the force that pushes up on objects that are in contact with the ground

supercross (SOO-puhr-kross)—a type of motorcycle race on a dirt track inside a stadium; supercross tracks are similar to motocross tracks

suspension (suh-SPEN-shuhn)—the system of springs and shock absorbers that absorbs a motorcycle's up-and-down movements

torque (TORK)—a turning force used to rotate or spin an object

trajectory (truh-JEK-tuh-ree)—a curved path of an object as it flies through the air

READ MORE

Adamson, Thomas K. *Motocross Racing*. North Mankato, Minn.: Capstone Press, 2011.

Mason, Paul. *Motorcycles*. Mankato, Minn.: Amicus, 2011.

Von Finn, Denny. *Racing Motorcycles*. Minneapolis: Bellwether Media, 2010.

INTERNET SITES

FactHound offers a safe, fun way to find Internet sites related to this book. All of the sites on FactHound have been researched by our staff.

Here's all you do:

Visit *www.facthound.com*

Enter this code: 9781476539126

INDEX